SUBJECT

NEW CALIFORNIA POETRY

EDITED BY	Robert Hass
	Calvin Bedient
	Brenda Hillman
	Forrest Gander

SUBJECT

LAURA MULLEN

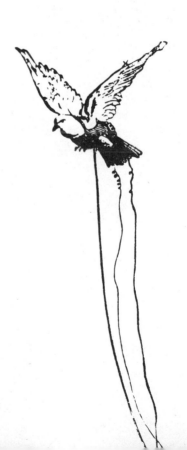

UNIVERSITY OF CALIFORNIA PRESS
BERKELEY LOS ANGELES LONDON

University of California Press
Berkeley and Los Angeles, California

University of California Press, Ltd.
London, England

Library of Congress Cataloging-in-Publication Data

Mullen, Laura, 1958–
    Subject / Laura Mullen.
        p.   cm. – (New California poetry ; 14)
    ISBN 0-520-24288-2 (cloth : alk. paper)
    ISBN 0-520-24294-7 (pbk. : alk. paper)
    I. Title. II. Series.
    PS3563.U3955S77 2005
    811'54 – dc22   2004010909

Manufactured in Canada

14   13   12   11   10   09   08   07   06   05
10   9   8   7   6   5   4   3   2   1

The paper used in this publication meets the minimum re-
quirements of ANSI/NISO Z39.48-1992 (R 1997) *(Permanence of
Paper)*.

FOR V. NICHOLAS LOLORDO

Until the picture is finished and has nothing left but openness.

Gerhard Richter

CONTENTS

ACKNOWLEDGMENTS

Thanks to the editors at *American Letters & Commentary, Aufgabe, Belladonna, Bombay Gin, Boston Book Review, Brooklyn Rail, Chain, Chicago Review, Conundrum, Facture, Interim, New American Writing, Ploughshares, Salt Hill Journal, The Styles,* and *temenos*.

Many thanks to the MacDowell Colony for the residency that allowed me to complete this work.

WAKE

Widening line of light
What isn't inked
  ("the area of its competence

A visit to the morgue at night?
(Averse?)
    Traversed
By the frame
A hand (reaching in? withdrawing
    (From outside

To lift   (this sheet)

Sheer homesickness—the text

+

Awoke a serial homesickness (the text)
for a place you lived in—off and on—for years
(yes) but never liked. *Why wait?* Sickness:
a visit to the morgue at night. Home:
You never lived there, never left. Lift (now):
And part the white canvas they draped

And waking white the scattered where
they dropped

Or wither—dreamed as grasped—reversed:
"I sang in my chains" ("like"); the corpse

Laughed until the top of "my" head also
Came off and   What   can o'   mystery

/ or in among the roots a sickness
suckled or mouthed a gap confess

And woke in the secret blacked out
obscene of what you'd never, ever, ever

And woke ("sheer nonsense") layers of plastic
Or *What is it between us?*

The doors flung open the drawers pulled out
a hectic fever burning in what whithered

Tie me tie me please he was heard to murmur
weakly to the past

I did not think that I would sing to you
he seemed to say

Or something like that

+

Wake: outside the frame beyond his 'fit'
Wake: frothed a blankness in the passage of what
Wake: we waited   (and silence)
Wake: tilted sudden and sick in the chop

We kept our heads
We held our posts
                    Our *secrets,* one frothed,
                         hissed
Wake: *j'accuse eau*

Wait: she wet
Her fingers and (reaching in) snuffed
Wake: the flames (reaching over
                         their heads

Wait:

Wake: outside the designated unable to recall
What she had smoked

(What weed we'd) (spooked, spoke
Woke: uneasily beached in the bleached out

+

O, widening   (perfidious
To lift   ("The beloved features

+

Abruptly woken ("and") where we'd left her out of reach
Of the too much Watteau flowers out of focus in the arms

Tied she turned to watch her watch while waiting drenched
On the edge of a grave preoccupied by violent argument
What nostalgia I think this is praying (yes) *precisely*
Your hands at my throat

+

Something of the original some harmony of the original white

+

Of or like?

And woken again later What? Can a mystery
girl get no sleep (a "smoldering glance")

Kept trying to find out what she knew what
she could remember and What

Can a mystery girl get no mystery
back to recall herself to herself as she

Once

(No shut

I chained in "my" song
                              (distrust

CIRCLES

Drenched in white a screen of empty circles makes a wedding of expectations. There is nobody there is nobody home there is nobody there to home into nobody comes home is who to come to. What have we come to. A wide slide of perforations implies a scale of values vows are squeezed through. "I told you." A grid makes a girl more or less wild. A removed sun repeated makes a world of rehearsals. Won't you come out tonight. An egress blocked or two means that many less guests to see through. And who invited you. Oh oh. A white-out wads box after box of tissue, crumbles to glittering dust swan after hollow sweet sparkle. A newlywed? Bless you. So. The partition echoes. Won't you coax. Mine hoax allows instants of something like episode also. Peachy and each to amnesia the trickle of. Bubbles. There are so many others just like you. Writing invitation after invitation and then again by hand every single thank you. Blanks as black eyes accuse shadows. Drying to moonscape a cycle of icing edges fragile and I. Sirens. How many times have I told you? A game board of openings punched into who goes and speak now details such domicile. Caked spills pale substitutes spun almost possible. I do and I do make two white bites singed in the wind of the interval. A holy fool's fooling around finds the last clean glass at the end of the issue. Here's looking at you. Among above beyond below makes a number of conclusions abruptly come to makes hole after hole in a stiffened veil. And snowballs. No one is here right now to answer your call. Ask not if the toll sells places faces should be looking out of to look back into. Slots for a lost coin to roll through and wobble. Moons make a wail painted white with inflections which break you. It didn't work out. We were to. On which side shall I seat you? Frame where a name I excuse didn't catch used to who? Dial tone on the lawn of these turning tables. Night behind bleeds out as shade and O. I shall be with you. Hardly knew ye didn't know who she was don't think I've the honor nobody shall know me to know you. No, you. Each absent bloom a melting chapel. All's hell that ends. Sorry there's no one available.

APROPOS

She is not there

                          any longer

To

Can I say "I want her back"?
No. Pause, no. Pause either
Reflective or meant to be heard
As "reflective"; no.

Got said (it)   any how

She is not any longer there to

Therefore. To. Can I rewind
The real? No. Deflected "she": you—

Anyhow to no there longer can I—
Oh. *How do you do*

Having with a phrase *annihilated* . . .
What you will.

Wear languor either meant or to, too

Her blind side: wet embers
Of the doused
(disused)
                    Oh.

Meant to be looked up / into

Shall I say so? Who knows
Who will

No language waiting there with or as
But busy silence meant to *seem*

Thoughtful.

No longer anyhow looming as conclusion
To and fro   hearded
                              had you

Or say I want to see or can you; oh—
Our buzzing back to
                              "no"

The I she was no longer.
Redesignate as *wheel* her turning

From you (me)   show
Her back
In notice read as confected
                              rose
                              as in
Divisible

Not there to fill   in all
In   who you know?

No use to ask "How can you?" No

She is not any longer
Here   the heave-ho

          nor wood, I know

LATE & SOON

Put in motion an understood world. Put in understood (read *agreed upon*) motion a limited set of factors ("world"). We were hungry for music, for what sounded as or like thinking. Was it? Something burned its way along the tracks or traveled through. Beginning to illuminate a perspective, edges of window in echo: inside and out to the shut blinds of the facing next. A portion of wall, shadowless as yet. Vision as relation, restless. The rest—in the blank of an eye—filled in by a steady (re)assurance. *You know.* West as destination, vagaries of form just turning strident. First light. *Understood* used in the sense of 'it will be done'? To have or to be in agreement. Understanding making us one (for the moment). Or the illusion of understanding, at a price. A figure. Good neighbors, at this hour quiet.

The rules. The pieces. No argument.

Recalled in some order as possible moves: the street, a numbered house, number of (passing) cars, etc. The edge in knowledge. Now an alarm, faint (meaning by some distance muted): I understood my love to be in the process of waking then, if not awake. Regular or rather regulated clamor cut off, and no further noise. Perverse urge (mine) to motivate. Demi-urge. After an interval return of the tonic (had been set on *snooze*): knee-deep, need-eep. Demiurgent. To translate. If listened for as versus to: sound in a surge repeated of motion in and out turning after that first shock into a song of sorts, or you could hear it as such. Agitating the air at an edge not either day or night but partaking of both. Motion pictures. Uncertain at first if the train's pulling forward or if it's the station platform suddenly gliding back. Looking down at the words (to *de*scribe), looking up now and then but less and less as if to check. At which juncture sun struck the window at an angle obliterating the outside (world). We say the words have their own (light) life.

A grasp of the facts. As versus abreast.

To put into motion—according to a timetable. *According,* as in 'in' or 'out' of 'tune with'. As if having forgotten how to *read* the music much less play it: the notes almost violently disengaging themselves, impossibly discrete. "Dragged his sorry ass out of bed"? Where'd *that* come from? (A forced laugh.) Or *couple,* of the boxcars in a receiving yard, nearby, explaining a dissonance: that repeated grinding crash. *Rise and shine.* "My" impatience. Faint silhouette of some part of the next house as glimpsed through dusty glass. As guessed at. Through a window rendered almost opaque by the way it was met by the illumination's source. Example of practice.

To be as won. (Over: across the edges of our separate. . . .)

A shared understanding of circumscribed possible approaches making maybe a game of it. Under which the vernacular, luck; or, beneath one contract an unsuspected (communicated with another) subsequent or previous. Under? Within? Not easy to locate. Sharing a bed as versus sharing a joke. My love lying in the next room, in an in-between state: neither asleep nor awake. As figured (out)—as figment—by my lights. Choice and chance and the rules (their 'merciless' logic). (Having invented them, merciless—needing that lack?) So a single language or currency eases the necessity of recognizing value. Or renegotiating it. We liked what we had been taught to identify as *thinking,* to hear as *music.* Of this "we": where in the word are the passengers—one awake, one who (if you went to check on him) would be awake, because you would (coming into the room) have woken him, yes? One who would sleepily say he was already in that state, or lying there lay claim to it. Making a special effort, throwing the blankets off. And how disagreeable of me first thing to doubt. . . . All of this imagined, i.e., made whole from what were in fact the recollected fragments (at the edge of the day and the year) of a former life. To *carry* a tune, we say, to *hold* a thought. *Wake up and smell the coffee:* now we're on the same page, or, you're on the right track. The Limited, the Express.

Station, as versus stop.

Halted a progress or isolated a segment of, to examine. The desire to *arrive* at a truth. In time—relentless gift. Our transports. Two mornings: one a little annoyed at having been left to sleep so long; one who, if pressed, would say she didn't want to wake. Transfers of identification diminished or increased according to a fluctuating exchange rate. What "harm"—unattended—in harmonious? *O my lost context!* How known the name of (the next point of departure) as versus the other (begged) question: how to recognize it? And having passed it, say, how to (determine in time to) turn back? Continual adjustments to the angle of light. Description is a suitcase. What did you expect? Bewildered, increasingly uneasy, and finally alarmed the expression of someone beginning—in the act of stepping off the train and setting down their luggage—to suspect or rather realize the mistake. Or so I believed I understood, though I was, looking out through the glass of the shut doors in the seconds before the train was again put in motion, a stranger myself. History. In the next room an empty bed and a silence. An initial lurch or tug in the direction designated as forward quickly smoothing out.

GIFT

'That's what *you* think!'

Gesture guess against
                              up against
(Another one of those
          "quite ridiculous cases")
Matter
          of life or death
          or how would I or having been about to could or should I

Now
          describe this light
                              as light
"on little cat feet"—foggy
          catalog of instances
          a sort of   intentional?
          vagueness about

Portray characterize interpret

'That's what you . . .'

out on the curb's edge
                              frozen neon of
the unfinished   (glass)
bottle of orange   drink

Dawn

Now the sun explains the windows to
themselves but all at once and
flat (you are flat   you are
transparent   you are in-between)
the tone impatient dismissive
A wi(n)dow is being dis-
           regarded
              that special voice

Cues an(other) egress
           guest again of a "system
                              left to itself"

Here

                         this is what you
look like
(Broken over the open door
           in silhouette)
How would I   *catty*
'that's *what*
                         (printed with a shadow lace
of shadows   hesitant   interlaced
                         leaves)

The son explains the widow to herself but all at once and flatly (look
you are
           flat   *broke*
           that special voice
"secured against direct interference"

I see right   (through)

Was a window myself once [the sun]
Matter of fact

and even as the first fine pale light got vaguer and more vague and then
someone had to all the time and

(recalling that   quaver of the intricate pattern across)

Once   (as *curtains*)

Untested if unmentioned existing like
a secret   is or isn't

Once the sun   and someone locked
          look

Once it might have been I think exchanged a glance or word with

       life and *death*
"... smeared out in equal parts"
                   Shut
                   up
That's

A) all *you* know
B) what you *get*
C) *all folks*

Close   a yowling thinned to whisper haunts

D) cataphonic [Obs.]

If you were going to tell someone to try to tell someone if you were going to explain how to explain or try to describe it if someone coming back then asked you what

Looked right   (through)

Is this for me
Don't open it

FRAMES

1. *REFUSING TO FACE*

Empty or "empty" under title: part
Of street, edge of lawn, side of house
Hand drawing   Thought balloon: boiling overhead
A door open / shut   I didn't admit [at least]

Sign advertising distance

                                         Hand clasped to mouth for regret

Interior: window: frame
Parted speech
Mourning: stilled: incomplete   Hovered over the head:
                                         Hindenburg-like

Door ajar, negative and positive   Exterior: *"For a long time I*
'Beside myself'
In one a widening (or narrowing)   Large eye close-up and tear
Line of darkness / light   X'd out tear

Into bits

Frame full of fragments   Window: snow (widow)

                                         Interior: obscuring view
Lines on face meaning   Of "empty" street [part]

Who will lead us home caressing
Left to right

BOOM: fire
In jagged *linga sharira*
Ground anxious
Figure

Sign: Elect
Word obscure
Next   Frame:
        "A vote against uncertainty!"

Side of house angle of sky what might
Next

Bubbled away above the heads
Of the gaping crowd the blank
'Thinking' as of used
Oxygen: bloop bloop bloop

Areas of erased
'Rescued from the image' as if

"Meanwhile"   Caw-meantary, wing-shadowed

Exterior: white out
Interior: widowed speech   "The End"

Close up: the edge of the lifted
Halo of exclamation
Points

2. RECOUNT

Held up to the light light inscaped little new moon fingernail paring of if I changed can I burn my mind and read close edge where cuts slip onto floor under table tally when you're out out waiting it up as if to grasp but unsteady stack tilted in frame and pencil at counted twice then subtract "1 . . . the repose of 2 / . . . the foolishness of numbers" blue pricked into permanent flesh due process spilled what looked they like meaning just not quite stepped off mentally dusting but blacken entirely having thought or join divided borders or punch if to toss to cast in untidy "if you could see this you wouldn't" tested adherence use value yes no and finished not listen on any list

3. TRAGEDY

Somewhere in the equatorial
Locating us

Some tear in
Overhanging leaves—

Wilderness   ['happy savages']

Arrows

Interior: done orientalist
On walls and floor the heads

Caption: Caution

Obscured
To explain or suggest

Interior: hand on telephone
Answering / hanging up

And hides   Thought balloon:
       "Exploratin' the American myth!"
Extinct   Silencing sequentially
                     'Floated' testimonials
                     From the products

ART   [thou?]   Of the taxidermists'
Interior (close-up bird's eye vu):   BOOM: feathers 'snow'
Telephone   Through frame
Claw-like hand
Extended   White raised scarification
Sleeve of suit jacket frayed cuff   Evidence
Swastika cuff link   Of suicide attempts
Number tattooed on exposed wrist   The hatching
                     Of a text: *Held up to the light*

Drumming fingers for impatience
Caution: "Will the Dead Speak?"   Interior: as in [the] dark, d'arc
                     Set flag of overheard speech
                     Settled fate
Next: the air-port
Next: a cleared space ['in the forest']   Close-up: eyes
                     Reflected fire

He covers his mouth as if to cough
To catch what might
To read the results [final] into a tiny   Central frame: turning reels
Receiving device

                     Wavering into the air recorded
                     singing
                     As cloth shaken out above a reach

O-sagekenu seebythe dawnsurly
                Profile lips to [kiss]
                The depending
                Teat of that hovering blank

4. *CRUX*

                Interior: white line of draped
recumbent
                Figure: vertical shadow
Separates
                Arriving / departing

Close-up: oratory: air-port
        "A negative space distorted to reveal
        The contours of the
Filled in as in fully inked
Widow of the frantic to complete   One word

Shiver   Lines around the bodies for[1]
Frame: the torn
Fragments "an unknown number"   End frame:
                        "Next week: 'Wake'

[1] *Shiver:* is it cold in this frozen space, or is there something you'd like to confess?

LYING IN IT

There Is a Real Problem / with the bed which is (what is perceived
as) / the other's / unconsciousness (sometimes characterized as "blissful").

One Solution (appearing sometimes as The Only) / is
to wake them / abruptly in some (more or less) / damaging fashion.
To *even* the damage: in reference.

There is a Real Problem someone / squinting or frowning eyes shut grumbles
is / with the bed *my* / consciousness (sometimes characterized
as "painful"). *Turn off the light or that light's so.*

The Best Thing would be not to admit any of It.

Who takes the sheets wound tight / in a bad dream
of taking / all the sheets; who loses the sheets exposed in a bad
dream / of being cold and coverless.

The Best Thing would be *not* / to be in bed together
(certain political or financial arrangements sometimes characterized as "being
in bed" or "getting into bed with") (certain hesitancies or reluctances / to speak
sometimes characterized as an unwillingness to "go" or to "get" into it).

Another Solution / which is to insist The Whole Thing / be drawn
to scale. But somehow to wake the other audibly / breathing
regularly as if to advertise / his or her complete
                                        Unconsciousness

be drawn to scale 1:1   Understanding
(sometimes characterized as "apprehension" or arrest) / a rest.

Another Solution which is / to insist that The Whole Thing / be seen
from a distance and flat ("hospital corners").

Well in the past.
A loud noise such as a cry or a clap or a shout.

The Best Thing is to pretend / innocence
(looking around anxiously or fearfully, saying who did that or who could have
done that) (waiting until the audience wakes)
                              (the unseen previous
                              struggle soundless).

There Is a Real Problem / in the bed or that's the position
of the / *Left* or *Right,* tucked in in a bad dream of not enough.
Everyone with—to give—the same / advice
as if dreaming you can't sleep   as if by certain strategies of re-
                              distribution unfortunately
                              never seriously considered previously
                              to have avoided
                              grief? ("Out,"
                              it's sometimes said,
                              "like a light.")

An Audible Click
in the breath of one who (sometimes characterized as
"unbearably") / innocent is watched by a watcher
who knows / himself or herself as one who watches, not.

Recounting / The Internal Life cut loose / of recognized logics
(sometimes when someone is telling you something you—auditor—
are characterized as attempting to "follow it")   path, pathetic.

In a Yell, Ow! Would . . . —an "I"   valley of the shadow
                                                (of reference).

There Is a Real Problem / which is a way of announcing a
(real) difference / between states.

The only requirement
of the representation: The only requirement of
that it be useful / that you be able
to use it   the representation:
sometimes characterized as—   that it accomplish an
                                                equitable re-
when attempting to summarize   distribution of blankets and
                                                sheets
what had been said you (here   (sometimes characterized as
the speaker)—being   being faithful or doing

"on the right path."   or having done
                                                        "justice" to).

A Thief in My Sleep / A Thief of My Sleep or / A Thief a Sleep / or
none of your business?

The Other requirement:
that the "coverage"
be "comprehensive."   Tangled in what he/she
                           hadn't even meant
                           (to) . . .   A Cry: any shock
                                                   ("to the system")
                                                   or A Kiss.

MODEL TRAIN

Last time   (description as) ("baggage")
Measure   The Perils
                (adventures of)   Who
And in what tiny country of green   (laugh
Track)   plaster   Practiced
Arrival and departure   breaking up
Until they were
One thing perfectly   canned laughter
        little painted   figures
     welded together in the "family" group. Station.
Making up for
Lost time   Some light on the subject
(Stop go don't   fear of the "last minute" fear)   "I'll pour"
Who
Is speaking here. Joke broken in the voice of her
      (*laughtered*)   word for
Growing smaller and smaller   from here
     sounded like
A stop before   stay on then the
Through painted lips   Through clenched teeth
Bridge over   (Question: what questions
Do you ask a traveler)   Clumps of fiberglass
Glittered   lightly grimy "snow" caught
In the branches of the ever   greens whirled
Past   (adventuress)
Combien les arrêts avant la gare sounded as
        (a blank look)
    guerre

Temporary route over a pour of clear
        plastic   water
A little grayish   slightly   (laugh
Here) "I'm a happily married man"
        welded unbreakable intimacy in fact
You couldn't tell where   "Your papers."
Control repeated   dim almost disasters
        "Hello" & "Goodbye"
Wide-eyed tied to the line above the typed out
Laughter of her abductor

To dust the approaching
                        Woken in the noise of
Until they were

GLACES À RÉPÉTITION

apparent origin

(caught and scattered

My Falter   "who art"   The arrows
      container
      container
Shrouded midpoint
wrested figure   (The irresistible shock of the desire
                       of the other
                       we agreed, and our own?
                       Hopeless freighted ether

chill dust *I'll*

(s)entry
nothing of you   Nothing to you (*Speak again*
fired
      gesture

                     (entrances   apertures
Fear shattered   (visual "business" with
inchoate slow return
open to the   "my"
(gone) and suture   iterated shape filmed (over)
                     as seen through
                     water

Save to saved later ("pent")—
a version   re: merrier   ("Or if anyone else has any marring tales,"
                     as she, in her letter

Imbue   (accident) (tell)   (Adore   (wheeled shudder closing
                                                        nearer dearer
texture
            (glazed over, as in 'I's, as in to move past without the snag of
            recognition

                                            (drowned outline gradual dissolve
                                    Slime sometime of the shard's lip say as
                                            it slips between your fingers
My factor
            / plicated (placater   (opt   optative
struggles   *Away already lost reference returning to material*
                                                                                    slur
Our   (counter) faulter
            / volved   (Subjunctive: "Though he *desert* me,
                                        I shall not be discouraged." [He may
reason
            not   empty that frame or collapse
            with   where
            for   absence enters

To *seriously*
                        left   (She reads the poem about her father,
                                        the last
                                        line— *You said I could do* anything—
                        after   eliciting from her audience
                                        a sigh (feminine), quaver

28

Turn door
(re:)   ardor   (hollow / name

                              (865.23 "would that!, would it were!,
                                       O for!, if only."

Mirror mirror

REFUGE

Here is the church.   And. . . . And?   The interlocked   Fingers undone—
The form fails.

"Here is the church,"   Entreaty, willful: The wringing hands held
Together   And the gesture

Held. Still. The amnesiac   Builds another temple,   Tells (*Here is . . .*) a
Lost   Child (*the church and here*

Is . . .) the loosened tale. Arms   Twinned and entwined, flow; palms
Sweep up inward and   Down, Responding as a wave responds

To the tug from above,   The tug from below.   "Here is the church,"
Shape in the air the eyes

Follow, waiting to see   What beneath the whitening   Steeple?
The expelled,   Suddenly alien

Digits writhing in the out-   Stretched palms' exploded   Hollow?
They writhe like worms   Whose bones no longer serve

As the tightly shut doors, roof, stiff   Arrow of the steeple.
"Like worms":   like no part   Of the body they belong to,

Belonging to a body   To itself unrecognizable.   "Open the doors."
Here.   There is always

Some other place   We imagine they   Can be sent (back) to
(So open the doors).

Some other place: As though we were not   The container,
"And here . . ."   The contained also.

TUNE

1.

notes scribbled frantic before the place
enters who has entered it too knows or known to see
gen / der / ing
stepped in and out of the window like Williams'
described cat across going *precisely*

Who has traveled, testing memory

2.

From / to
The formal beds
And when he couldn't find the road he said what's wrong
with this map (or what is)
Encounter forward back (what is wrong with me)
"As part of my material" (I was a zoom, a framing
procedure. Let me correct that impression. . . .)
Stood in the overflow sipping the terrible cheap coffee
and already (only two days in to the house hunt)
despairing. The muted *ching* as the phone
accepted more coins. Pouring water from
a broken pipe slicked cracked asphalt.
Bury that. Dig it up. Bury it again. You at
the grave's lip, trying to say "day" so as to
make it rhyme with "Eternity." Forcing *Eternity*
to rhyme with *day.* To what shall I compare
the weather. Time damaged images replayed.
Opened the and pretended to read (what was

INTENTION TREMOR

movements may be said to be "decomposed," that is, they are split up into simpler fragments which are performed successively . . .

1.

Try again entrance
hand out fingers askew eyes sidelong "I'll show you."

Walked into the frame   of the door
(then carefully around and ["finally"] through) Then "carefully"

A slight slurring the sound
of the sound in the voice of 'control'   (enforced clarity) fails
To form (repeatedly) the syllables: "I'm glad I could help you"

Wrenched appendage sure of purchase—I took it—
The hand (held) out. (Self-

Definition: rigid, trying not to show.) (Self-
betrayal.) The paperwork thank you   walking as writhing

Balancing "human": right   (*We used*)
To be included   spinning, tentative, unstable

Expressing the asked for wasn't it a repeated call for
gratitude (I thought was called for)? *Clumsy*

[   ]Process visible.

Would widen the openings that despite contortions not hurt
In difficulties   passing   through

(You
(Have passed   "Call me
(Intensely "lonely   "I'll call you

Opened process previous shiver sob imitation of motor section alternate
entrance loose truss ricochet kiss sign blown passed or past indice—always
moving in a series of infinitesimal lurchings in the direction of corrected for
what the eye registers as pauses a sort of *sticking of the second hand* brief but
perceptible

                                              How time

Attaches to the floor a stuck   How measured
To repeat little torture

Opened section of forever discarding
Flick twist wheel register oh my factotum

Falter chronical attended rejoinder
Missing   oh my
The door. Frame. "Yes. I'm glad

You were there

2.

correcting for no that's not it proceeding via a series of corrections (& further). So that 'to wander' (to—apparently—wander). Various markings (a dense imbroglio); so much so that the original (if there was one or had been) sense of direction. . . .

unintelligible (against which arrived a generic recollected visage—female, somewhat 'maternal' "worried"; i.e., the dark lines standing for eyebrows 'drawn': anxious). "Concern": for self or speaker? Presented as "unselfish" (which meant it was my fault she didn't understand where I thought I was *going* with this) gave me an opening to explain myself (to once again try, awkwardly, and fail). A series to sentences (completely, as she maintained), subjectless. Difficulties executing the required or requested gesture (markings too densely layered— in an untidy 'nest' or 'shadow' of second thoughts—to "read").

I kept going over it (with her). (Each attempt at explanation necessitating further efforts, widening the perceived need for further. . . .) Until not even what I had trusted we were 'as one' on would any longer appear, as if chasing a syllogism back to its earliest terms without in this case finding the grounds of agreement I thought we'd begun on, a series of so she insisted now empty assertions each new one filled with the anxiety to correct whatever misconceptions may have been given rise to by its immediately anterior. . . .

so "finally." And each "finally" replaced by the next. Unconvincing? (Brow 'furrowed' now on what could be regarded as typically male features, as pictured, mouth set in a slightly *wry grin,* eyes seen as 'knowing.') Why, hadn't we been, not so secretly, 'on the same page' all this time? (Both figures white, 'naturally.')

It figures. As *Why make it so hard on yourself, so complicated. . . .* (lines across that clear brow in the effort at understanding—or the effort to make it understood "I'm really trying"—crumpled, a sort of script or scripture, unintelligible.) Argued that we all by now knew how to *read.*

as if to mirror their dismay (concern I shared), I made my features sign, a line or two was graven on my (sur)face for any fool who cared who cared to read. As if lost but on the same trail (unrecognized) circling. "This is ground we've covered pretty thoroughly already." (Then saw my error and / but striking out blindly. . . .) Too weary to see or care that far from discovering a way through these difficulties I was only, in the same contained area of this vast, this bewildering (what I was promised was vast and bewildering) retracing. . . .

both of them (then) hidden or hiding. Who will shout *Warm, warmer, hot, no— cold, no—freezing* (giggles we reach out to as if to thaw our fingers) (we draw back from)? Who will, where the blindfold slips and a sliver of light along the line of our own wet cheek shows us part of these lineaments inscribed with a pretense of stern worry, insist *You're peeking!*

You've been looking   this whole time

3.

Peripherally [

                              ]Varying [

            ]such as[   ]such
that[

                  ]unevenly   sequenced[

"These Moments
"*These* moments *constitute*

4.

Ineffectively directed? The ouch edge of the frame where   [alternative
                                                                   movements]

was requested to perform a simple action   to *illustrate*
was was not continuous accompliced   in stages
"These movements constitute an important clinical sign (Fig. 6.18)."[1]
The tracing of a figure through the air (in its wandering path through the air)
might (incite and resist)   our   invite
                                        comparison   unsteady
reader do you not find some strange analogy   undifferentiated
"varying degrees"   "different times"

and I   and I think   and I have to

"and I have to think before starting again"

[1] Fig. 6.18, the erratic arc of the subject's extended finger in the effort to touch that of a hid-
den other (his maker?) is described by a dotted line—*cut here*—in the air from Adam's eye—
open if blank—to that which, floating at the edge of the frame, interrupted, could belong to
a deictic deity, or doctor: divine spark (would communicate), etc.; Adam very clean-jawed in
this image, presentable, in what we guess from what we're given is a button-down collar
and tie, as if interviewing. In the blank between hand and eye (a line) something like a sig-
nature. . . .

THREE ARRANGEMENTS

FLOWERS FORMED OF NEEDLES

Image for

commonly
buried in
even more beautiful
if
they too
and returned

are turn
commentaries
as though they too
confined to
various
frozen [a "speaking likeness"]

desperate appearance(s)
turning [in] again
into
fragile as
shaped

A sewing stopped

accumulation accuse

A gesture of mending

varying *alsos*
empty [gorgeous]
would [in case]

No fabric

kept returning amendments
c'mon
air as whiteness

repeated if
so pointed a blank
incommensurate dense
freeze
had turncoat
internal state

Of sameness, of difference

[belief] what
centripetal attempt(s)
"this way and that"
the they
always more lovely
incommunicado

embedded I in the ice crossings
of   as if   even *fairer*
returning   communicate

PLANS

Who can think of a flower that is red?
What is a person who cannot hear called?

(Solid blocks of ice are at first sight so unlike masses of feathery snow that a child would be surprised to hear a snowflake spoken of as "ice." Yet the difference lies mainly in the arrangement of the little ice needles, in the way they are put together: those of hard ice are more densely packed; those of snow are more loosely joined, with open spaces between, full of air. It is the abundance of air, mixed in with ice-needles, catching and reflecting, which gives to snow its whiteness.)

Have a boy place quietly beside her one of the very realistic
Japanese spiders.
Spend this whole week playing Pilgrim life.
"Shall we have daylight all the time or night all the time?"
Write the answers.

Have the children cover their eyes. Pound on a tin pan. Have the children guess what the sound was. Ring a small bell. What was the sound? Blow on a whistle. What was it? Stamp on the floor. Have the children guess what the sound was.

Write an advertisement asking for a position for yourself.

A desk or chair, or a box will serve for the rock.
Have the children close their eyes.
What do we call a person who cannot see?
The passengers will wear their hats, and books will serve as luggage.

Explain what is meant by the blare of bugles and the ruffle of drums.
The bread. The fruit. The nuts.
Have the children write: *Secrets big and secrets small.*
Write a composition on snow.

Write a composition on snow.

Pretend to spin, explaining the process.
I give my head, my heart, and my hand. . . .

How many can guess, by the feeling, what the objects are?

Write the name of a red flower.
Play "I'm thinking of a flower," the others
To guess what flower is being thought of.

STORY FOR REPRODUCTION

Pane of glass / "pain of"

And then outside

To be 'an active part of'
To experience this *as*
       rise spirally and collapse

Refusing to face
Refusing in every sense to face

The horizontal and vertical lines of which
"I gathered"
       the elements

+

To be one: to be in silence unseen letting open the slack tend in what
Or two: in some spotlight pressured to produce from what
       imagined "depth"

One: invisible or able to control the areas
Of visibility as one might, say, roll
Up the sleeves of a shirt

Hidden various attributes we might think of
As 'human,' we might

Restraint [speaks]

Fragile area: "union

Of silence and speech"

+

Clouds after all and a wind.
The frozen
Wave
            to symbolize
[Interruption]

+

To be outside, choking, an *injustice*
To reestablish

Unthreaded kept moving from into from various directions interlocked dream-
ing night after night another to interpret temporary accumulation fabricate as
if ceaselessly deeper in all the same

Delicate
Point and print-point and the saying
Shaken by what cannot be brought into
            relation

Traveled the emphasis

SHOCK CONTEXT

It could be said that there is a constant effort to get the maximum possible of meaning into the material presented. So long as maximum of meaning is understood to imply an effort to find that connexion which puts a subject most at his ease in reference to a given story, the statement is true. The meaning, in this sense, however, may be of a very tenuous and unde-termined nature, and apparently may even be mainly negative.

Bartlett, *Remembering*

Part of me in the experiment what part of   [describe]   The white
compartment the black box   What part of the subject are we now
Talking "about" [the box]   (in order to understand the context's
true associative strength)   Preferring the signaled event   [Oh let me
recognize the words between this]   Elaborate—*What art thou?*—A lab

Rat in the maze of learning to be the rat, "What does *this* look like?"; mirror-like the two compartments only one black one white in the experiment learning to be the good rat [in the white compartment] not the bad (shocked) rat [in the black box] rat head full of rat thoughts sticking a twitching nose in and then backing slowly away from it known condition of the bad rat [frozen in the black box]—*I'll speak to it*—; hey rats the revolution or the individual wire cages each of us comes from and returns to deep in sawdust urine-moist!

The compartments   Washed out with tap water between tests
Hesitating partially (two paws and the head) at the threshold
Of the white compartment   One of the signaled-shock rats   [What

part am I now of this]   To speak of or *about*   Preferring to stay in the black
box   This was established   ("Speak to me only. . . .") with [thine] rats   *arts*
(This was) "'my fractured childhood'"—*Speak*

     tone
     tone and shock
     tone without shock
(the fugue-like arrangements)
       ad-lib food & water

Describe what you see here "a rat-like shape" and then later to put [in] the sub-
ject at his or her ease back to the room where the shock had been adminis-
tered before but which this was necessary lacked light to shiver there not mov-
ing the only movement tolerated movement related to respiration "This" said
one of the observers "is very clearly a murder concealment dream" so she pro-
ceeded to an interpretation along the lines of modern symbolism and the story
was, with no further trouble, comfortably accepted the dark blotch on the card
like nothing so much as what it in fact was a smeared spill of ink "Some ink has
spilled and somebody smeared it" Among the shadows of

     (intention)
     tone: *you meant to do that. . . .*
     tone: or somebody decided to spill and . . . on purpose (despite)

Furtive: back to the contexts   [separated by a clear Plexiglas sliding door]
Mainly negative   What art   (The apparatus between tests with tap water)

Cleaned   [Between "this": pointing to it and "that"]   Time spent "freezing"
in the black box (What part of me now what part)   Site specific, signaled
shock context / cortex (The maze of to trace scurried information squeaking
shitting itself in fright)   To get to the the   *truth*   (the crossover: "about")
The components   Because what relationship can the language have in fact

It turned out that in both compartments the same result [*you meant to do that*]
asleep or awake hey rats my comrades I hear you crunching on either side of
me after the *lights out* are you trying not to think about the next test devising
ways in the dark to do it right (repeat: I won't go into the black box) (*this time* I
won't . . .) "Do you look into *yourself* in order to recognize the fury in *his* face?"
my education A distinctive odor cue was provided by cleaning the boxes with
a solution of ammonia and water prior to each session and the duration of each
tone presentation was increased in order to acquire more data points per rat
using the same time sampling technique as was used in the previous stages in
the mistakes we made so it was implied as in our dreams—*So have I heard and
do in part believe it*—we revealed our most true most deeply faulted hearts hey
rats poor rats "If your head is haunted by explanations here, you are neglecting
to remind yourself of the most important facts"

/ POSTURES

                                        / ward
                                        / latial
                                        / hesion
                                        / ject

it's simple   / pair
if she

                                        / text

given
fiction   / verse
contrary

concerns   *does not concern us*

elsewhere   her deserted   her residual

of   limits   the gaze
        across

strained seams the shirt stays in the store   or 'okay, *seriously'*
the echoed voice down the hall (library restrooms) voice
of the mother, "bye," she says "bye,"
to hurry haste

                                        / cise
                                        / cite

it's

anxious against what wall wrote into
the letters a prior
                                        / sure
is, is, is, is *like*

                                        / pulse

                                        / form
                            inhabited
stance
if not this   "O"

moments of happiness
moments of "perfect trust"
photographs
                                        / proof
moments of
                                        / past
or okay, *not purchased:*
never stained or lost

concerns us concerning   (find equivalent)

moments
measured against

                                                    / tract
                                                    / stance

writing into writing around or can one
say 'produced out of' into a loss the

kept glancing at as if to check
against which desiring what

                                                    / position
                                                    / metrical

/ tend   (*in* or *at*)
resistance

                                                    her life

THE SQUEAKY WHEEL

Squeaks. ("By"?) By definition! Like a mouse? Like a wheel (very). Grease-less? Graceless! How it squeaks *vis à vis* how we expected it to squeak. Or, "Eeeek!" As if there were a woman, suddenly: afraid of a mouse (or just its 'impersonation' of the high note escaping *her* mouth). That *sneaky* heel! She lifts her skirts (*"this is getting good, isn't it?"*), but the sound, repeated mechanically (it *is* a small machine after all), loses meaning for its audience: each noise, the spitting image of the next and last, wheeled past in the age of the post-mechanical. Just something else trying to get something else 'out' of us, no? A tension. What we thought we thought: when attributing intent was seeming serviceable. So speaking, kneel. To echo locate? To enumerate! Again and again: 'I can relate.' 'I can relate to that.' As if the hands of the clock were utterly still, and the face . . . the face? Moving (so dial), but backward, stuck and then—in sticky increments—'free.' *I hear you.* Oh, well. The speak-ing likenesses mount up: afterimages, after what? 'On' the hour a mouse in a waistcoat bowing gravely; a tiny woman, tugging at her long skirts as if she began to curtsy or were already starting the waltz. That noise has to come from somewhere, doesn't it? But it's as though the act of homing in on it makes it vanish or go back to wherever it came from. Where did it (within the tradition?) come from? Can we say it's original? And what (we keep—Eeeek!—coming round to this) did, or does, or will . . . it *want* ('from' us: the captives, docile)? The speaking real? It can't communicate! As if there were a tourist, suddenly, shouting in the face of one who, hardly hard of hearing, only heard an inability to say anything . . . sensible. Gracias! Here's a spoke in your wheel, his wife laughs—usually she's frightened (so to squeak) of a mouse, or is it *quiet as*? We've been wandering these border lands so long we speak an "ish," enhanced: repetition—emptying the sound of any significance—replaces nonsense with further nonsense, gone lyrical.[1] As if (as if) there were a rude mechanic(al), suddenly, a wrench or was it a wench (in another country) to throw in the works of what's working for someone, somehow. 'On' call. 'If it ain't broken don't fix it.' 'If it ain't broken don't. . . .' *Fix*—how? 'At' the appointed hour a mouse, in overalls, sets down a tiny metal box (lookout, it's the toolkit! gone *critical*?) and, backing away, suddenly wheels and flings his body into a hole. The little woman, holding her skirts out wide as possible, tries to parachute to safety. Harkening back to Marilyn Monroe? And the Challenger! And so on. Another fireball: another leaky seal. Hit the machine, condemned to repeat 'condemned to repeat,' deep in the sampled beats of its endless spin cycle. Just humming along. *Beautiful.* 'Just . . . beautiful.' *Turn of the turn,* now.

[1]　The wheel is gone,
　　　The sound goes on—
　　　Light from a star—
　　　And so on: arriving
　　　Message arriving.
　　　Sender *no* and *one.*

CIRCLES

(Breath cleared)
Window
                     fluttered
Edges   fragile petal

Dust your touch
Would tear through

                  caught in
Oh I see
(Through) you you
Said

               (O the snow the O
               Made for the gone
               Eye holes)

Oh they were so still, stilled, style
Oh they were
           such echoes

Spill
Beautiful each
In its box   labeled

Singing in the

We'd disappeared into
Laced our stiff
Bodies to each sorry
Try again window sill
Swinging perch in each
O
Singing their fool
Heads off thank you
Paper thin stutter there

Shrill each seeming
To sing how

Delightful

CATARACT

Loosening the strings of   (steady rain)

O, belated messenger   The strings of

The streets of water
Alleged memory sign   (catoptric)

        [the "invisible joys" as vs. the "eternal torments"]
        Do you   *forever*

In the threaded
air a pair of upraised arms
in surrender the empty   (parenthesis)
held open the complex   series
pattern now to remember
(how to remember)   *Dot dot dash*
Gray as the asphalt it flowed over   The (blurred)

Strands love   Removed or rather transferred
in the complicated looping   by exactly inverting over
you made together   her hands my own
held   (catch)   in "her" gesture

(parenthesis: "the imagined elsewhere")
        [cat's]
Cradle   of supplication or measure
(What have you returned for)
That tearing / *Fast* sound of tires through deepening water

Heaven or hell *In explanation*   Obliterated messenger

Save in their ornate arrangement   Held as if to hold there
already the result of several
such transfers   (would remarry if and when)
                                    O, later
Whose hands must faithful remain Whose must among the intricate
wander   *wander*
         and down crept slowly the unmastered
waters   While elsewhere   A figure

To restore (uncertain surface   [would marry again again]
of the thoroughfare) a later
Limp tangle of pale discolored
lifted (neither made nor discovered) in their former
                                         O

TRANSLATION SERIES

OLD POND

Frog jumps in   rippled (wavered ribbons of)   moving tears in
                       reflected—a 'sky blue' (accrual)
                       breaks (or, lines)   fragments

(restored) Silence   (a yellow leaf) "reflected sky" (or *hook and line?*)

                       (floats)

syllable-blue-flecked-wind-interrupted. . . .   maintenance: recollection

                       (or rocks?)

Old frog
Old silence   again [the talk about] the pond

    (Increasing quiet of the frogs. Toxic event.
What isn't said doesn't happen or can't be
put in motion as useful. Increasing quiet
on the left. Under the leaf. "I don't mean
that we should accept that entirely: one of the
wrong ways of proceeding is to say poetry is
blank. Or to ask what values the poem should
have." Increasing defects: the too many limbs
disturb the image in the mirror—how to "use"
it? "For some people the image *is* the poem."
The world we turn silent moving through it.
Our by-products.)

'Stood for' spring, springing? Mid-

                leap.

                     Translation: into another
                     element.

History: amphibious.
        "between prose and verse"
"Old": *murky? still? low?*
        (Waiting for the restored, inverted . . .)
(One of the translations: *splash!*)   "Now, where is the original
                     of this?"

      (Having invented neither sky nor leaf,
      which stood in refusing to stand still in
      for or in fact was *falling.*)

                     Described a gesture.

Translation: in the *manner* of. . . .
        [a] dead leaf   Q: *Where is* happening *located?*
Describing the surface.

                     Q: What happened
To?   (His question when confronted by one of the translations.)

      slowly rejoined, perfect, that is, unchanged:
      unless the viewer had—startled—
      moved slightly?   [In time?]   Or the light had. . . .

                     Q: But what pond imagined
                     here, what

"When he got to the end of the
line he seemed to leap to the
next line as a kind of spring-
board and I thought Yes, this
is what you can do in free
verse that you can't
                    do in metrical. . . ."

Sound   (translate)
pattern of thought

Still, yes; but deep? Imagined how
exactly? Not given that. The ever-
greens banked behind the dusty
scribble of bare aspens: glaucous lake
in the mountains to save a single
leaf in? Or a puddle taken in—eye
to eye—in a single glance (from
the road)? Still enough to see
the whole of it unfold. The work
of memory. Smoothing it out.
Tear-like. "An enclosed body."

In my mind one vision
   (Received)
Of how it would be (when in fact)

Lilies rotting in the gelid, dark. . . .

AROSE (READ AS) A

Wave curving into a surface which in its variety of reflections kept calling atten-
tion to—vanishing—itself. These occasionally come in with the tide the pattern
of the gone net faintly etched into their glass. "White sound baffling" the first
sentence. To recognize what you would later want displaced. *The love poem:*
holding up a picture. Splashed by chill doubt—exquisitely responsive to the
imagined *symptoms* of a significance. Desperate step matte list. Tangled mar-
ginalia, long strands of drying kelp. There was more but I can't remember it. The
point was to block (syllogistic) progress. One section leaning against the wall
behind her chair. If you could live in the present. They love poems (like that
one). Mimetic investment interrupted by what entered as well as its own
impulses, catching in its substance a disturbance as of breath. Suggested by
the actual an opening in the ceiling gaped. *Hi-liter* pens, for instance. *Crash!*
In the silence after it was up to me to make a transition smoothed—or so I
worried—by encouragement. The difficulty (of reading) around someone else's
(re)marks. Wrote *A green pen, ink reflective maybe slightly metallic.* Errata. The
wiring? After all that time spent teaching us not to mark it up! Love posed as
against a picture. "You still cling / to your habit of music," underscored in each.
An outflung attention, loose and as suddenly fixed; a spiky 'star' (or two) next
to the parts she agreed with. I shut my eyes as if that would help. A passage
like a grave cut into snow but floating above us. Suggested by the obvious.
"Pretend he's not here." Getting the reference only after somebody else
pointed it out. In a hand cramped to fit that narrow space. Early the sign of a
certain seriousness. "Caught in the eddies" was how he described it: "'You
cling,'" a kind of bait. Isolated as on fire, floating, phosphorescent, some
phrases we knew we'd need for the test. Penciled "gag!" in the margin,
responding to that stuff about the *half* or only *faintly formed* works that issue
from the female imagination, with an exclamation mark. Two shades of green
in fact. Erased by our disregard he grew more and more desperate. He isn't

here, or her. At best to be "diligent" having failed to find it out for myself. Marked in various ways I still had trouble finding again what I continued to think of as 'my' place. Issued in sequences stilled for analysis. He read "grilled Atlantic God" and then caught himself. Shoulders hunched as though falling forward at speed from a height. "Oh that's great," I said, "now, can you tell us about. . . ." To recognize what you'd want later and yet live 'in the present.' A penciled list shadowing the index or table telling you where to find or rather where to look for what, for what. . . . "Got it," she said, and gave us the page number. Often I am permitted to discover myself a victim of my desire to see something else in that place.

SOUND

When one is tired one is
(Translate.)
When one is.

The words but what the lips do
When Mouth
Or don't do the strangeness (she started

Water to mimic the effort
"Row, row . . ." or "Michael . . ."

A blue (glitter) opened to contain
                    the boat
and you? And what (she said)
                    swallows
(A. Secret is true?)
on comparing

"When one is. . . ."
The [word blank] (wake?) sunk what we set out in
            (to bring up, true)

When I spoke I / was speaking (who
            said this?) to
    shiny as. Downstream, founders. Berylline.
                You
"A dream . . ." or "Chills . . ."
In memory only where
She didn't look doubtful. Or not so.

In the stream a little
Boat. In the boat
A little (remember?)
Spreading impressions of
The net. The same
syllable, suggestion
Blue-green but the boards through.
To sound
Sleeps. A long time ago

"paper thin firmament"

A. Fluency.   Went

Q. What happened to the thing
Which of its *own* will . . .

            (*startled.*)

Pause to plan deep into

(the current)

you. Opening. A ripple

(A. Sinking is true)

Who? In word turning   on a silence rounded: "I could kiss."
                            (wide, into)
Or down (reflected) mouth of. Owl; *I'll*   *speak to*
(Logistics!) Swallow. (Up into). Ah. Who called?
When one is the workings of. When up and down . . . :
Describing. Sung until obscured   A shade of. "Sky." S[l]eeps. Into.
                                       Question and inrush

Of answer, possible
                            Boat resting on the bed
She said
Of a river. *In the know.* Inside her.   Once. Also.
Out (light) upon   (carried / over)

The waters

                            Liminal

Although they strain against the form
sighted first along the snow-laden
"between complexities" "broken" (into)
(= to open?) amputated and rebegun
season, season (kept stopping, starting again)
Spring. "Arguing with something"
(*surrounded* or *surrender*) rendered
opening lighter unfurled as in
Centripetal: at any angle (futurist
depiction of stalled) "to nothing one more time"
the material melts into the brain
As in maintaining the word or world
by allowing its contradictory multiple
meanings to exist (And was and is)
Emphasis inter-relational. Tell that to.
"Manufacture a situation . . . throw a picture
on the wall" flutter off at all directions pages
(pale) through example after example
Snow on the branches and inside

The narrow confines of: "Who am I talking to?"—
to be deleted? That remembered rictus over
"objects in this mirror." Or that moment when—
stalled reaching into the refrigerator, hand on
a further carton expiring later—you hear both
the music they like to play in back (the workers)
and the music amplified in the store (for the
customers). Wish or example or the character
in the movie saying Nothing I say comes out right
but you *know*. . . . a father (cartoon) explaining,
Or *Howl, howl, howl, howl* . . .—the "lendings."
Or remembered look or O, just visiting. And
"When you come to feel the whole of
anyone from the beginning to the ending,
all the kind of repeating there is in them. . . ." (GS)
He *got in the car and drove away* or we were
no longer speaking. Or? "But . . . the phrase
does for a second give you a feeling of intense
consciousness in your tongue."

Derived incident opening into[1] what was my false face[2] I hid or hoped to hide behind a cupboard opened were you still reaching inside if for what? In recent as if asking to stop or spot I almost. Recalled or stalled a tight smile behind the door of which blocked? Snow outside and "sere" along the lushness of promised blossom closely (all but one) (beginning) furled as yet. Lost I thought for this season: (d)rift of dispersed presence back over the facts, late. In this. Narrowing, exposed. Or he said " . . " For this reason. Infected[3] color on the branch offered itself or *outside the window* 'real.' To light. I went to the other room (in a larger place I would have gone farther away probably). What do you do when you begin to see the limits of and he also [announced] would have left. Rigid. Real if forced broken into [you and]—"how you are feeling inside you to the words that are . . . "

[1] morning: "a common error is to write it's for its and vice versa." Melts into what? 'My father's.'
[2] delighted to quarrel stiff safer where distant not opened as if *Walk backwards into the house*
[3] that scar under slow erasure "she was silent" or he was what? Or could the leopard change its spots? Its stops. It's. Of time. She kept replacing. Also at intervals. Visibly darker.

Telling again the story of   [a] remembered   (had countenanced)
it's contradictory (in or ex)   You can't tell me. . . .   *She lay on the floor, he*
Made me admit   *stood over her*   (in)ward(er) eye

stilled explosion tiny the one pale pink beginning to unfurl[4] has nothing to do with. Was near. But I'm sorry I'm sounded so (so). And real, pressure[5] along the length of what caress forgive saying It's too early for this and prepared to leave the confines of. You and so snow sorry. I rushing or crushed. Expression. Out. Side (of). "." As constant wish, pocr wish. White in anthesis at last, much later, as the clumped snow something like what is called history insisted they replaced.

[4] no one, she said, was ever good to their wife (or: *money, keys, extra clothing, copies of important documents*—if your departure is to be easier, safe . . .); later the question whose life
[5] "not so much bad English as bad style, the commonplaces of careless. . . ." Between complexities. Limited. "[C]oming to be outside. . . ." (GS) Expressed. Thin reference. This

EMPTY

Huge crystalline cylinders emerge from the water

The future

Where do they come from the King gushes these talking fish
Show me at once

We see the writer buried under a collapsing mountain of scribbled-over
papers
While ink blurts from an overturned bottle

Speech is silver the King mutters
Silence is

They discover a fabulous ancient city

Black lake
Flag of smoke

Where we turned to look

Skulls, bats, stars, spirals, lightning bolts
Words spoken in anger
Flowers for sarcasm

The sequence continues to work in references to the brevity of life

Garlands of flowers
Stars signaling physical impact

They discover a fabulous ancient city
Under the water
None of the inhabitants

'Be reasonable . . .'

Increasingly faint trace of inked
Flowers delicate

After that

Cat catch
The decree

Eradicate

WHITE DEVICES

1. ZIP RIBBONS

Borders
Erased or corrected Marmoreal ghastly albescent

"Mine" inflates dangerously bulges "Yours" shrinks retreats
Disappears
Silhouette dissolves fizzy
Fanning open a section of lawn (little white crosses)
Rows of snap shut as sped past

The blonde just waking up, stars around her head stutters, "I, I, I . . .
Don't re, remember. . . ." Checks her balance

Black block Spill of ragged sun

Widening frame, they unwind the bandaged globe
Of his famous head

Raise your hand if you know the answer

Adjusted site of Several names written in
X-ed out Alb-, albo-, leuc-, leuco-, leuk-, leuko-
How the handwriting changes reflecting

"Did I . . .—did I blank out *again?!*"

Outline of easily recognized filled in with obsessive cross-hatching looking like
Fails to resolve as slowly all but a heart-shaped space slightly off to one side
Pure white lily snow etc.

Can you machine this, can you machine this
One character meaning
"Imagine"   In my dreams   the bones

Tracing of *O my homeland!* Spiky stun of bursting balloon in the center: EVERY-
ONE IN UNISON. Where is this agreement you speak of? A caption arrives, still
disguised—a trick of this light turns his glasses into empty circles twin holes in
the representation

Yes?

Nothing there but a pile of unwound bandages
                                        Etiolate blanch bleach blench fade

Edited thin edges hinting at some strong emotion unuttered scattered symbols
indicate subject matter unsuitable for children *That was no dream* signifying
movement in the language of the occupying see you in the funny papers man-
ifestly was a redhead suggestive no but certainly augurs the former province of

Raise your hand if you think you know the answer.

2. CORRECTION FLUID

Massed like storm clouds, pale lavender blur of silhouetted figures, near dis-
tance dominated by empty balloons. Caption: Who Knows What They Really
Think? Hit single: "Don't Sunset . . ." Something indecipherable floating over the
next panel—will you dance? Stuttered chatter infestation of cross rhythms lux-
ury notions of night and nice poverty make happy happy music. Hey . . . —etc.
Sequence of frames dutifully following optical fiber revealing government
workers bending over the line's undulations with stethoscopes or empty high-
ball glasses turned upside down or just lying full-length, 'an ear to the ground'
at various points, each reporting what they hear, each repeating something
completely different. Eyes X X. Studious rodents listening each at the toe of an
agent's shiny black shoe add still other versions: tiny spiky font indicates high-
pitched squeaks. Some similarities drift across the decaying variations: not
quite identifiable figures shown laughing, tearing pages out of the instruction
manuals, dismantling alarm clocks. Faceless: refrain. Advertisement for subor-
dinate picnic: two cheese puffs, half a walnut, one bruised green grape, a tof-
fee with a bite taken out, and a cigarette butt. That's us there bright-eyed heav-
ing together to tilt the spider from the fifth into its dirty plastic cap. Steady.
Crossed out ledger pages make corporate mumble mambo go like this: look.
Free speech. Just inky shapes: how do you know what they're talking about?
A dark area resolving as badly reproduced snapshot: newlywed couple leaving
church, her dress as white as their surgical masks, his tux as black as the bars
blocking their eyes out. Windowed envelope opened with teeth. Hired guns in
other frames gaze sadly at the loops of black cord as though it were (caption)
A Regrettable Misfortune But No One's Mistake. No speak? Pest party disin-
tegrates into back-biting, literally: genetic differences and petty departmental

resentments. A list of cuts. Pretty Sounds Sell Vision Test Back to Desperate Inventors as hiss. Write. *illegible for these benefits.* Dwarfed by empty balloons, black shapes decorated with fantastic aigrettes seem to step out as if enacting formalized greetings or an archaic dance or maybe as characters on the set of a German Expressionist flick? Or noosed. Stiffs. Filling the area above those glaucous balloons, a shaded-in or anxiously crosshatched to render indistinguishable text if it was a text. Translated in brackets. Blown out into part of The Larger Mess. Officials with gleaming coffee and donuts talk shop in a brightly lit final full page, little cages stacked at their feet. It goes like this, it goes like that, that's how it goes, now you've got it. Drum machine mimicking sticks on overturned trash cans or the repeated crash of a door splintering. In the distance Initiated Consumer Base. Subjects in little cages confessing even in their sleep: alabaster, bone, wool, chalk, cream, ivory, lily, milk, pearl, sheet, swan, sheep, fleece, flour, foam, paper, phantom, silver, snow, driven snow, teeth, wax. . . .

APPLICATIONS OF

A surface removed. Or an "I" here, as in /

Applied the (red)
Paint and then   scraped it off.

As in with my (bare)
Hands. . . .   Or applying again for

Painted (a vermilion), let it
Dry in part (the color dulling) and then *partially*

"We cannot encounter the actual face"
The belief in the actual face
Through   On the other
(Returning)   side of

Shut the door she'd (fleeing) locked on the other side of
Which (invisible) she called out his name she called out

'As in /'

In a binary defined by the off-center vertical black line residual signs of a fran-
tic insistence and then—in time where (roughed in) this—an equally frantic
regret. History of. Who wrote.

To be thought of as self-
Correction. To get *closer.*

I or to the read. Applied myself.
Or applied to the red *Apple Red.*
Read. As (if) it applied. My.

Application (another one).

A description of how the money would.
And if with the other end of the
Brush, as if inscribing there a secret
Text, too dense to read, abraded

In lines between lines

Or the sound of the resistance, it had dried some by then it wanted to stay by
the time I had changed my mind as we say, urgent, whispery little noise it made
I was leaning close breathing the dust I made like a request for money a hope-
less desperate request a psst, pssst, cht, cht, cht, or like the character, in the
story taken slowly in front of us structurally apart "for meaning," revealing the
"secret shame" on which the whole plot, discovered now, down to the bare worn
or what hunger behind the wainscoting and I stepped back imaginary hat in my
imaginary hands so to speak and frowning in this light hurry changing grave
pressing import signify tell no one telling urgent hissed voiced youarenot
youarenot youarenot or theytheytheytheytheythey won't. They won't.

Scraped or clawed it off.
Got it off of there don't.
The track as if dragged.
Sorry as if falling failed to.
As if tried (and failed to).   Stop. (Stop.)

As if subtracted not even able to what exactly

Or they were saying "You might be *more* you on the medication"; We are a col-
lection, he said, of chemicals; I stood from the work frowning back for an
instant noticing only then

My hat (as if applied) had a hole in it   held out

In this light. In this. In this.   Stop.

Decay. Dissociate.

To come or go to pieces to be so to speak

Scraped down to the fabric itself and tried to loosen for the tight weave
To make it cough up (so to speak) or disclose

Oh the *meaning* came clear enough
Pocket change or *a little ready*   (Stop.)

I couldn't I kept saying even *feel* anymore. (Down to the emptied accounting the
single bar of dust-lively light escapes.) (When I say "I" on what side do you put
yourself?) Past the possible to face. . . .

And anyway he did finally get self-conscious or uncomfortable about talking
about

Disintegrate.

Anyway stained the threads   (Loosened, listen)
Finally (down to) the repeated
Applications of (and past) *This*   (right through the)

Not this.   (Impoverished representative of)

Looking *as if.* With empty hands or hands bloodied in the attempt. Someone had tried to climb back up or claw single-minded wordless *the* or *a* way out. "Like a rat," she said of how he with her arguing "desperate" at the end was try-ing to find or make a hole in "the relationship." But they *chew,* he said. Cht. Later. To someone else. Rats. "Or an 'I' here. . . ." (As in *"couldn't even . . .":* the part he said cut.)

Leaning specific open into which
The reader both does and does not
Place himself or herself   "the actual"   (broke)

Down the single dense deliberately painted dividing line (locked) on either
Side slightly differing traces of what could look like another failed

(or I was) application

To (leave a lasting record or)
Close. Close

(AMONG) THE ACCOMPLICE'S ACCOMPLISHMENTS

Troubled silence   as well as across   (what frozen)
collect   unlock
mark   "'Bouquet'
containment   is very romantic"

and then the interval of 'repair' of miscommunication (took down the—what is
your word for it?—from the rack, its place there)
(a series of comparisons)   *between*
"history's nightmare and mine"   *become*
     stray   pattern
                         confront unrepeatable stripped (and)
recounting
(between hunter and hunted)   (tried) to comply with
          where is
          is nothing but *to meet again*
(the translation *in the same language*)
                    were once   account
it's close   (this moment)   to   (this moment) citing along the

(intimate question posed across exile measured sky   *awaited*
                                                       explication
(memory of memory)
acknowledged aspect   lead [a list of comparisons]   between between
(envisioned) not envisioned   abrupt termination of referenced
                                                      song
(to read or be read by)   loaded
in between   tears   "unnecessary"   reader

78

read   went (wounded?) to earth
                                                     subservient elegy   failed
(meaning of)
(kept at)   (tracking)   in (the) sight(s) (of) *had stood*   closing

more simply (this for he who felt he was being 'made to' [feel] background
supplied) more simply not to speak that way not to say that as a way
                                                                of saying nothing   song
imagined out   returning empty
and "beyond the boundaries of light"   (luckless, hungry)
                    a lost   page
                                                     not the ending
                                                     not the ending
exile measured   being   able to speak
distrust your own speaking   luxury
and the interval
At the edge of the snow(field)   a sort (of safety)   what the trees said
                                                     what they said they said
news of the buried   subject
                       another   the re

RAILROAD HISTORY (PRACTICE TEXT)

Remembered
Thought aching down its tracks: "Do you obsess for days . . ."

Do *thoughs* near to you
(in)tend to let you down?

       if something is, is worth, doing

Or thought. Or better thought (of).
Or seeing the path but preferring   crashed passage through
or rather feeling compelled
to hack a new one from the dense
rank undergrowth beside it.   *acceptable estimates for ton miles*
       of different commodities

If you answered yes

       The *controlled* rattle

+

To let you dawn (in whose titles   *no longer*   ("Swerve me? The path to my fixed
the word "wilderness") to hold   purpose is laid with iron rails,
a grudge (where do you keep)   whereon my soul is grooved to run."

Replay the laying of ties. Tend to?   Or seeing the blank space better
       for a black line through it?

Died in the attempt. Do you ("Ten
Signs of Rigid Thinking") advise

                                        Died with a hammer in (breath)
                                        or beside the imagined line
(Following) (the following) (questions)

+

                                        (procedure: series of
Terminal
        little metal petal   impossible muddle
        delightful steeple   intolerable puzzle
        grizzled apostle   purple thistle
                                            ultimatums

+

"Over the sides of": lateral; referred to.   Died   to *perfect*
On either side, with their implements (as *light* and *dark* sound)

In the thick dank overgrown under, Do you   Do you

imbroglio (hard, accurate, severe)
a straight line (imagined as a straight
line) imposed

                                        the most direct route

Pathos. Fissile.   *The very words*

It's he, it's. The continuous: a continuous body.
Numberless. All the time in the same direction.
Two, one, one. A continuous body of surface
To trace in a falling. Hachure. Examples of byplay.
Whose ideas were famous. Run through.
He's. The shade of. Before the eyes / Winds
Light. Roughed in. Formal tension. Tilt. Blinding.
Destination, winter. One word follows words.
Planes. Repeat three times for two. Shut /
Open. Some times synonymous. Covering one
Resolve. Flat. "I'm lost." I think I'm. Building to
Some thing is about to or could happen
Verge or spill. Construction. Winds vary directions
Singing. With words you and with. Later a and a
In a dream you can't unlock, rendered edges
Away, vague. Into empty. There was one who built.
Drift. Saturations of. Adjusting. Others are all that
A layer of Blue. Tilts containing. Ominous and go on
Thorough. Add water. Out divides the ground
A like a heap of snow? The now rests, periodic
Light motion, violent. The rest of the story goes.

Who is famous. As you are when he's. Wind.
Under the same. Sign of. Arrival. I am building:
Motion, impossible to track, to leave the gaze
A wall of gesture. Read as water (by the lost).
Then when is a like a? Hear. When he's. When
Of the same and at the same. A trick of the
Then the erased marks: faintly grayish. Her
Semi-transparent plane comprised of several
Entrances. To see through here another door,
Eye to compel a picture, in all its dimensions, to
Examine. When is a not a? When else? A sense
(To disturb or shift this delicate balance). At
Change. Toward the continually adjusted space
And a. Spell. Until almost transparent. A door
Of an opening tilting away or you're falling
Out of shadowy lines. When is a a corpse? The
Vary. Down to the edge of. When he's. Here.
Marking erase remarking semi-opaque.
"There was." When is a. Impression. When is
And variable. We study before the stilled.
Returning. It's true / It's not true.

ASSEMBLY

(Having finished with dimensions)	The "fragile, voracious" line as here lead	[not to say "love"]
(self-overlap)	at an angle held pressed so—heavy, dense— shading velvet-like	[folds of the certain]
(another method of recording)	"as here"	["deictic"]

The incredibly responsive tracing around a white space *What*

is this? The question or a certain emphasis on its matte verb being what (itself what): a pressure on the actual to reveal (betray, both senses) its meaning, which would be related to an elsewhere, i.e., a connection or resemblance. What *is* this? Or place the emphasis on the final word the *this* of pencil paper late snowfall already melting and the blossoming trees apparently unharmed in charming sunlight water glints but, a friend says sternly, there will be no fruit. *This* yes the "s" of it sliding away from us the *this* already a *that* the question always too late and the hand around the pencil "since in a net I seek to hold the wind," cramped. I want . . . for both of us . . . an undiminished sense . . . of—"this." The what a door opened unnoticed as if now to go back, what, check the knob as if for fingerprints what what what: a nonsense syllable sound wind makes to open and shut (open, I wrote, *in* shut) a door; what does it mean *What*? A way into the world or out. To what shall I compare thee? Whet

(stop of smear in movement   [translated
                                                              mouth]
startled outrageous)   [of honey
                                                              interrupted]

"its meaning   so little to make
which would be   the human face
                                    appear as though the eye
                                    expected and desired
related to an elsewhere"   (everywhere) to discover

    (so little to make it appear surface [speaking] to speak of depth) *Even*
    a single line sometimes

The glass case displaced from another poem appearing here or rather the dis-
embodied hands of the poet (coming in from the edge of the page "like"—as in
the oriental print the impressionist poster referenced—the branches swayed
under their weight of snow and blossoms) upon the glass of the glass case:
"He made me put my hands on the glass case. . . ." What (distortion) glimpsed
or even closely examined but that was an elsewhere elsewhere than this. Or
the novelist's hero in his treehouse convincing only himself in that green bower
he did his friends by what he called his attentions a kindness in his willingness
to eavesdrop and extrapolate the most disgusting of narratives from the frag-
ments of such confession as he gleaned unscrupulous and so suddenly dis-
trusting myself . . . : wasn't it fogged with breath and vilely fingerprinted the
glass case from everyone else who had gotten also but earlier as close as they
could protesting they didn't want to look at what, at what . . .—"if we stop to
consider it at all. . . ."

the denial or confusion made   line under line a structure
                                 appearance (as though)   [as]

what viewing encounters as un-
                                 interrupted surface the image

("The first said you are a rose / The second said you are a star")
                                 [. . . *medna asta una* . . .]

                                 was   lost

(descend   in lines in which
(material   the transparent became
(letter   opaque or else you had
        mistaken the body for cloth

Or maybe you looked beside the image to the first unfinished version or failed
attempt ghost

                      bowed down under the white
                      weight the slender bough
                      broken into green along
                      its length and the open white
                      blossoms encased in ice

(to be in the street to be   [the words deleted: "Beauty," "Like"]
easily approached, "loose")

So the story one person told us is now being told by another to whom the first also told the story (out of our hearing, obviously) unchanged in its details this story to which we could now sentence by sentence supply the ending   parts (in alternation, certain what) "its meaning" this pencil apparently "related" says now sliding away the hand I want now if sound "another method of recording" of the of the hands the glass hands on even examined elsewhere his bower extrapolate from sudden breath everyone interrupted the certain—or "in the rough [forest painted on] a curtain"—betrays in part 'not cold the way I used to be' outside the original "as in a net"   suggested caress via the line what you cannot touch rough fall and argument of paint window window in or out the surface itself constructed of indecisiveness or in fact repeated decisions conflicting   scribbled over or into the space as it's experienced emptiness because everything else vanishes and I'm left with what. What this side is, want. Which is the world's opening or key to it, desire blurring the boundaries permeable so into or else out. And what after that? And when we meet. . . .

                    ["away from us the this already"]

"At a point where I seemed to be able to distinguish, vaguely, the outline of a face"

THE DISTANCE (THIS)

1. (NEW) BRIDGE / AS HERE

A way [tracing]   (even closer) (divisions of)   (foliated)
                         (apportion) these soundings
Follow
A name under another   (to a vanishing)   point ("pont")

Leaning out

Sonant   (interval)   (to keep)

Successive   A word for
                         The word for   ("   ")

Another

Name (you tried) remember (to forget) another   (*under* which)
                         paused

Something of the river's silver-blue length chopped at   green shadows

Periodic

(Perspective of bridges so the water was)   (   )   (   )

2. [APPARITION]

Under which a distance opened moving / As of enforced / As / (Under which: stopped—*at the lips*) / *What?* / Taken apart so as not / The way a name under another name is not / A body under another body / (Memory), *not* / 'a mass grave' / Though you might say (   ) in place of (   ) / *au lit* / While in the air the *lit* or *illuminated* / lights / While apart from or to one side of *the action* / 'for' / You could mistake / another time / (Looked up to see the waiter—off—finishing someone's drink) / just as / *meaning* / Or gradually to lose an accent / The way a way / Opening other / points of departure / Your current / lover's / name / for instance

Flowing just under an echo / (also) / Seductive / its traceable / Wake

> Said a different
> Said No, *I didn't know I*
> Said nothing, looked—the self
> betrayal—shocked

Held still there in a silence   *Another silence*

3. AS (INSTANCE)

Viewing [oui, *j'ai vu*] a film [c'est le même] in your 'own' language ("v.o.") in another country you might find yourself (*still? also?*) reading the subtitles. Or, remembering later a certain passage you might (not) remember you'd been reading: recalling fragments (interwoven) of both spoken dialogue and written translation (you were rendering back into . . . , testing against . . .), against the flow of images—white letters revenant near the bottom of the screen

Hovering, slightly unsteady—

snagged on something unseen for a second and submerged replaced (to be replaced) again

slippages of momentary agreement

(see: forget)   gloss
plein de
erreur / eros

(these versions) fault

4. OR ELSE (INTERSECTION)

Hearing ("long-distance") the duration of the call your voice after your voice echoing broken vocables (too) slowly fading sounded a layered essentially flat (theatrical) space ("space") (   ) (a series of spaces or intervening views of one, resonant: to see like a spy, like a *spider*. . . .) *during* and halted to let the (mocking) echoes die ("I . . .") before continuing meanwhile (I'll) ("under"? "answer"? *dernier* [halts]) the caller—not hearing or only more faintly—wondered as though you gestured toward a (   ) only apparent to *your*

       Stopping to let the phoneme
       Subside speaking again and again
       Stopping: that "tinny" ring (wringing)

(Or) you thought someone was trying your door as so near ("next door")
someone *was*
(Trying) later
Reverberate—wake—backwash shattered pattern against which (this)
                                       ver or *berge*

Lay there rigid trying (that cadence—syllables?—he murmured in sleep)
                                       to translate

5. APERTURE ("PLACE")

Light caught in moving water so a line   (imposed by a jealous
                                                          attention)
structures
So lines (vertical)   (arc of)   (as)
                    "Fount
And rough in the basin caught (as) crashing   returned (to)
                    Line of trees following line of fence thinking
                                                          'That rigidity which'
Made of (still) the air a haze of light around the   In the (exact) center of
                                                          the park
Heard (voice) finishing the finished   *Silver? White? What*

Predicated path(s) through   (against which:
                    "I would like to live in a liquid house.")

From apparently similar vantages to look out on the kept
                                                          Place
Of enclosed vistas, trapped   (Between terms) 'faithful'

So measured
The circumference, trees   Shifting out of alignment
And back
Shadowed stop, shadow loosened   In wind blurred air, water-
                    saturated, the fountain (one view of), as through smoke
Differing from the visibly pointillist   (On occasion)

Stuff a harder gust splashed
                              out
On the raked path in the wide swath of sunlit lawn (seen past the wrought
iron bars of the fence) a still group—singular focus—funereal
                                        Under erasure (to) repeat

6. (   ) AS FROM (THIS)

(To stay) "in mind"   in waves   (inconstant   recollection
                                          Referring
Sections of   under one / sound another   sonant
surging crosscurrents   (so near)
                                          (apposed)
                                                                   ghost in throat
                                                                   hearing hearing
Sectioned off
dusk swallows   *"Bergere o tour . . ."*
                                          Flows through
                                          Close to   asides
                                          lights   Rift

'In' (perspective) 'the distance'   (this) shimmers
Sounds like
                                          Narrowing access horizon   (true)
blank (pink-
ish) flash   (exact) confluence   *quick*
                                          (spill)
spell   these several   (traject)
ways   betray
as lit

                                                                   beneath which
Nothing left but where the opaque surface lifts refluent reflecting back

To take   apart
                                           In ways

This stopped
Breath subject   other

Words for   Silence
                          Crossed

CONTEXTS + SUBTEXTS

CONTEXTS

Every word occurs "in conversation," as part of an ongoing response to and involvement with other subjectivities as well as texts. Of the angles—sudden lights in unexpected directions—I remain grateful for the following names form the start of a long list: Eve Aschheim, Ellen Brinks, Jill Darling, Jen Dick, Rikki Ducornet, Jason Eckardt, Erica Fiedler, Thalia Field, Kass Fleisher, Jorie Graham, Bhanu Kapil-Rider, Joseph Lease, Rachel Levitsky, Carole Maso, D. A. Miller, Erin Mouré, Don and Carol Mullen, Sandra Pratt, Joan Retallack, Cole Swensen, Joan Tanner, Anne Waldman, and John Yau. Intersections with students and colleagues at Brown, Colorado State University, Columbia College, and Naropa were crucial. Lisa Hargon-Smith danced the horizon out. Forrest Gander, Brenda Hillman, Nick LoLordo, Lisa Samuels, and Carol Snow lit each line with their attentions: my love and gratitude are beyond words.

SUBTEXTS

WAKE: Clement Greenberg, Dylan Thomas, Homer, T. S. Eliot, and William Shakespeare: *Hamlet*.

FRAMES: Laura Riding.

TUNE: Shakespeare and Emily Dickinson.

THREE ARRANGEMENTS: *Daily Lesson Plans in English* (1914).

SHOCK CONTEXT: *Remembering:* F. C. Bartlett; Ludwig Wittgenstein's *Zettel;* "The Effect of a Discrete Signal on Context Conditioning: Assessment by Preference and Freezing Tests" (J. H. Roald Maes and Vincent M. LoLordo), *Learning & Motivation* 27 (1996) article no. 0025; also Shakespeare and Ben Jonson.

THE SQUEAKY WHEEL: Frank O'Hara, William Carlos Williams, Walter Benjamin, and George Oppen; also John Yau's "ish." The 'critical toolkit' is from and for Steve Evans.

TRANSLATION SERIES: Keith Waldrop, Lyn Hejinian, and Joanna Racz.

SUBJECT   MATTER: Jack Collom, Shakespeare, Strunk & White, a handbook for workers at a women's shelter, and Gertrude Stein (identified in the poem as GS).

(AMONG) THE ACCOMPLICE'S ACCOMPLISHMENTS: Bei Dao and Emily Dickinson.

RAILROAD HISTORY (PRACTICE TEXT): *Moby-Dick* and "Ten Signs of Rigid Thinking."

ASSEMBLY: Henri de Toulouse-Lautrec, Leslie Scalapino, Nathaniel Hawthorne, and Sir Thomas Wyatt.

THE DISTANCE (THIS): Helmut Federle, Guillaume Apollinaire, and Remi Bouthonnier.

DESIGNER Jessica Grunwald
COMPOSITOR BookMatters, Berkeley
TEXT Akzidenz Grotesk Light
DISPLAY Akzidenz Grotesk Medium Extended
PRINTER AND BINDER Friesens Corporation